ACHIEVE **WEALTH** THROUGH **MINDSET**

Achieve WEALTH Through MINDSET:
Unlock your earning Potential & Design your Dream life

by

Andrew Henri

TABLE OF CONTENTS

PREFACE	1
INTORDUCTION	3
• Unlocking the Code to Financial Freedom	3
• Cracking the Mindset Vault	3
• From Scarcity to Abundance	4
• Roadmap to Riches	5
PART 1 – DISMANTLING LIMITING BELIEF	8
CHAPTER 1 – THE MONEY MONSTER	9
• Belief Buster 1	10
• Belief Buster 2	12
• Belief Buster 3	14
CHAPTER 2 – REFRAMING YOUR MONEY STORY	17
• Unearthing Your Money Script	17
• Rewriting Your Script for Success	18
• Building Confidence	20
PART 2 – CULTIVATING WEALTH-BUILDING HABIT	28
CHAPTER 3 – THE FOUNDATION	29
• Unleashing Your Potential	29
• Overcoming Limiting Belief	31
• Embracing Abundance Thinking	33
CHAPTER 4 – GOAL SETTING	37
• Set SMART Goals	37
• Creating Your Wealth Blueprint	40
CHAPTER 5 – WEALTH BUILDING STRATEGIES	45
• Invest Wisely: Stocks, Real Estate & Beyond	45

- Leverage Passive Income Streams - - 47

CHAPTER 6 – FROM SPENDER TO SAVER - 53
- Mastering the Art of Financial Discipline - 53
- Budgeting Basics - - - 54
- The Power of "NO" - - - - 56
- Building a "Pay Yourself First" Mentality - 58

CHAPTER 7 – THE COMPOUND EFFECT - 63
- How Small Habits Lead to Big Riches - - 63
- The Seed of Wealth - - - - 65
- Daily Money Wins - - - - 65
- From Latte Factor to Millionaire Maker - 67

PART 3 – EMBRACING ABUNDANCE - - 72

CHAPTER 8 – MINDFULNESS AND MONEY - 73
- Develop a Healthy Relationship with Wealth - 73
- Wealth is a Mindset, not a Number - - 73
- Beyond the Bottom Line - - - 74
- Gratitude is the Gateway to Abundance - 75
- How Generosity Creates Prosperity - - 77
- Managing Money Mindfully - - - 79
- Balancing Wealth and Well-being - - 85

CHAPTER 9 – TAMING THE FEAR FACTOR - 87
- Making Smart Investment Decisions - - 89
- Understanding Risk Tolerance - - 93
- Investing for the Long Term - - - 94
- Building a Diversified Portfolio - - 95

PART 4 – MAINTAINING THE MOMENTUM - 96

CHAPTER 10 – STAYING MOTIVATED - - 97
- Understanding Obstacles & Sticking to Plan - 97

- The Power of Positive Self-Talk - 98
- Celebrating Milestones - - 100
- Building a Support System - - - 103

CHAPTER 11 – OVERCOMING CHALLENGES - 105
- Resilience in the Face of Adversity - - 105
- Navigating Financial Setbacks - - 105
- Overcoming Fear of Failure - - - 107
- Building Resilience for Long-Term Success - 109

CHAPTER 12–MASTERING THE WEALTH MINDSET **112**
- Tools and Techniques for Lasting Prosperity - 113
- Visualization and Affirmations - - 113
- Practice Self-Discipline & Delay Gratification - 115
- Surround Yourself with Success - - 117

CHAPTER 13 – CONCLUSION - - - 123
- Embrace the Journey to Financial Freedom - 123
- Reflecting on Your Progress - - - 123
- Committing to Continuous Growth - - 124
- Inspiring others to Achieve Wealth - - 125
- Remember You Deserve to be Rich - - 127
- Living a life of Abundance starts NOW - 128

PREFACE:

Welcome to the world of limitless possibilities, where the keys to financial abundance lie not in the depths of your bank account but within the recesses of your mind. In this groundbreaking book, **"Achieve Wealth Through Mindset"** we embark on a transformative journey to unlock the secrets of wealth creation, empower you with the tools of mindset mastery, and guide you towards the prosperity you deserve.

As the author of this book, I have traversed the landscape of wealth creation, navigating the highs and lows, the triumphs and tribulations, and emerging victorious with a wealth of knowledge to share. Through years of study, experimentation, and personal experience, I have discovered that true wealth is not merely a product of external circumstances but a reflection of the inner workings of the mind.

In these pages, you will find a treasure trove of insights, strategies, and practical techniques to cultivate a wealth mindset and unleash your full potential for financial success. From the power of positive thinking to the science of goal setting, from the art of visualization to the discipline of delayed gratification, each chapter is packed with actionable advice to propel you towards your goals.

But this book is more than just a roadmap to riches—it is a call to action, a challenge to transcend the limits of your comfort zone and embrace the possibilities that await you on the journey to wealth creation. Whether you are a seasoned entrepreneur, a budding investor, or simply someone seeking a better life, the principles outlined in these pages will empower you to take control of your financial destiny and create the future you desire.

So, dear reader, I invite you to embark on this adventure with an open mind and a willing heart. Together, we will explore the depths of mindset mastery, unlock the secrets of wealth creation, and chart a course towards a brighter, more prosperous future. The journey may be challenging at times, but the rewards are beyond measure. Let us begin.

~ INTRODUCTION ~

Unlock the Code to Financial Freedom

Are you tired of feeling trapped by the paycheck cycle? Do you dream of a life where money is a tool, not a master? If so, then you're on the verge of an incredible journey – unlocking the code to financial freedom.

This isn't just about having a fat bank account (although, that's certainly a perk!). Financial freedom is about *empowerment*. It's about having the resources and peace of mind to pursue your passions, travel the world, or simply live life on your own terms. But before you embark on this exciting quest, there's a hidden vault you need to crack – *your mindset.*

CRACKING THE MINDSET VAULT

Let's face it, our thoughts about money are often deeply ingrained. We might have grown up hearing limiting beliefs like "*money doesn't grow on trees*" or "*the rich get richer, the poor get poorer.*" These messages can subconsciously hold us back from achieving financial abundance.

The truth is, wealth creation is a journey, and the first step is *reprogramming your financial DNA*. We need to move from a *scarcity mindset*, where we see money as a finite resource, to an *abundance mindset*, where we believe prosperity is available to everyone.

Here's the key: When you cultivate an abundance mindset, you open yourself up to new possibilities. You start to see opportunities where you once saw obstacles. You become more confident in your ability to manage money and make sound financial decisions.

This shift in perspective is powerful. It's the foundation upon which all your financial strategies will be built.

From Scarcity to Abundance

Imagine your financial reality as a vast, fertile landscape. In the scarcity mindset, this land appears barren, with limited resources. But with an abundance mindset, the landscape transforms. You see fertile fields brimming with potential, waiting to be cultivated.

This shift requires a conscious effort. Here are a few exercises to get you started:

- ***Gratitude Practice:***

  Focus on what you already have, be it a steady income, a roof over your head, or supportive relationships. Gratitude attracts abundance.

- ***Visualization:***

  Take a few minutes each day to visualize yourself achieving your financial goals. See yourself living comfortably, debt-free, or pursuing your dreams.

- **Affirmations:**
  Repeat positive affirmations like "*I am worthy of abundance*" or "*I am a wealth magnet*" to retrain your subconscious mind.

  By consistently practicing these techniques, you'll start to see a shift in your financial paradigm. You'll move from feeling powerless to feeling empowered, ready to take control of your financial destiny.

THE ROADMAP TO RICHES:

Now that you've cracked the mindset vault, it's time to explore the exciting roadmap that leads to financial freedom. In the coming chapters, we'll delve into practical strategies like:

- **Budgeting & Expense Tracking:**
  Understanding where your money goes is the first step to taking control of it.
- **Debt Elimination:** Crushing debt removes a huge burden and frees up resources for future investments.

- **Saving and Investing:** Building a nest egg is crucial for achieving long-term financial security.
- **Income Generation:** Learn how to create multiple income streams to accelerate your wealth creation journey.

This journey won't be without its challenges, but with the right mindset and the practical tools you'll gain in this guide, you'll be well-equipped to overcome them. Remember, financial freedom is not a destination; it's a lifelong adventure. Are you ready to unlock the code and live the life you deserve?

PART 1:

DISMANTLING LIMITING BELIEFS

~Chapter 1~

THE MONEY MONSTER:
Exposing the Myths & Misconceptions that Hold You Back

Have you ever felt a strange tightness in your chest when you think about money? Does the pursuit of wealth conjure images of ruthless tycoons or penny-pinching Scrooges? If so, you've likely encountered the Money Monster – a sneaky creature lurking in your subconscious, spewing financial myths that keep you chained to a life of scarcity.

But fear not, brave adventurer! This chapter equips you with the tools to slay the Money Monster and rewrite your financial narrative. We'll expose the most common limiting beliefs that hold people back from achieving financial freedom, and dismantle them one by one.

Belief Buster 1: "I'm Not Meant to Be Rich"

The first belief we must confront is the insidious notion that some people are destined for wealth while others are doomed to a life of mediocrity. This limiting belief undermines our confidence and prevents us from pursuing our full potential. But the truth is, wealth is not reserved for a select few—it is accessible to anyone willing to challenge their beliefs and take inspired action.

Consider the story of Sarah, who grew up in a family struggling to make ends meet and internalized the belief that she was not meant to be rich. Despite her talents and ambitions, Sarah's limiting belief held her back from pursuing her dreams. But through introspection and self-discovery, Sarah realized that her beliefs were not truths but stories she had been telling herself. By challenging her belief and adopting a mindset of abundance,

Sarah transformed her life and achieved financial success beyond her wildest dreams.

This pervasive belief often stems from childhood messages or societal conditioning. Perhaps you grew up hearing phrases like "money doesn't grow on trees" or witnessed family struggles with finances. These experiences can lead to a subconscious belief that wealth is reserved for a chosen few, not for someone like you.

THE TRUTH BOMB: Financial abundance is not a birth-right, but it's also not a lottery ticket. Wealth creation is a journey available to anyone willing to learn, work smart, and cultivate the right mindset. Think of successful people you admire – did they inherit their fortune, or did they build it brick by brick?

ACTION STEP: Identify the source of your *"not meant to be rich"* belief. Was it a specific comment or a general atmosphere? Challenge this belief with evidence of everyday people achieving financial success. Research self-made millionaires and create a vision board filled with images that represent your definition of abundance.

Belief Buster 2: "The Rich Get Richer, and the Poor Get Poorer".

Another common belief that holds many people back from pursuing wealth is the belief in a zero-sum game—that there is a fixed amount of wealth in the world and that for one person to gain, another must lose. This scarcity mindset breeds envy, resentment, and a sense of powerlessness, perpetuating a cycle of lack and limitation.

This cynical belief paints a bleak picture of a rigged system where the wealthy hoard resources while the less fortunate are left behind. While there are certainly inequalities in the world, this belief fosters a victim mentality, hindering any attempts at financial progress.

But the reality is far from this belief. Wealth is not finite; it is created and multiplied through innovation, entrepreneurship, and value creation. The success of others does not diminish our own potential—in fact, it can serve as inspiration and evidence that wealth is attainable for anyone willing to put in the effort and take calculated risks.

Imagine a world where every success story is a beacon of hope, where each triumph inspires others to reach for greatness. By challenging the belief in scarcity and embracing a mindset of abundance, we can break free from the chains of limitation and unlock our full potential for financial success.

THE TRUTH BOMB: The reality is more nuanced. There are countless examples of individuals overcoming socioeconomic barriers to achieve financial security. The key lies in focusing on what you can control – your own actions, skills, and financial education.

ACTION STEP: Shift your focus from "getting rich" to "building wealth." Focus on developing valuable skills, creating multiple income streams, and making smart investments. Remember, wealth creation is a marathon, not a sprint.

BELIEF BUSTER 3: *"Making Money Requires Sacrifice and Suffering"*

One of the most pervasive beliefs that hold many people back from pursuing wealth is the belief that making money requires sacrifice and suffering. This belief perpetuates the myth of the "starving artist" or the "workaholic entrepreneur," painting a picture of financial success as a distant dream reserved for those willing to endure hardship and deprivation.

The Money Monster loves to portray financial success as a lonely pursuit, achieved only through relentless work and self-denial. This belief can make the very idea of pursuing wealth seem unattractive.

But the truth is that financial success is not synonymous with suffering—it is about creating value, serving others, and living a life of purpose and abundance. While it may require effort, dedication, and perseverance, the journey to wealth is not one of sacrifice but of fulfillment and joy.

Consider the story of James, who believed that making money required sacrificing his passions and working endless hours in a job he hated. But through a shift in mindset and a commitment to pursuing his passions, James discovered a path to financial success that aligned with his values and brought him joy and fulfillment. By challenging the belief that making money requires sacrifice and suffering, James liberated himself from the shackles of limitation and embraced a life of abundance and prosperity.

THE TRUTH BOMB: Financial freedom can unlock a life filled with freedom and enjoyment, allowing you to pursue your passions and spend time with loved ones. Think of wealth creation as building a strong foundation for a fulfilling life, not a prison sentence.

ACTION STEP: Redefine what "sacrifice" means for you. Is it giving up unhealthy habits that drain your finances? Perhaps it's prioritizing learning a new skill over mindless entertainment. Focus on sacrifices that empower you, not those that leave you feeling deprived.

By dismantling these limiting beliefs, you've taken a giant leap towards financial empowerment. Remember, the Money Monster thrives in the shadows. Shine the light of truth on its lies, and you'll be well on your way to unlocking the code to financial freedom.

~Chapter 2~

REFRAMING YOUR MONEY STORY:
From Lack to Limitless Potential

In our minds, our beliefs about money form the very foundation of our financial reality. We all have a story about money – a narrative woven from childhood experiences, societal messages, and our own observations. This internal script shapes our financial decisions and ultimately, our success. The problem? For many of us, this script is riddled with negativity, filled with messages of lack and limitation.

In this chapter, we'll embark on a journey of self-discovery, unearthing your money story and rewriting it for success. Through unearthing our money script, rewriting empowering beliefs, and building unshakeable confidence, we pave the way for a future filled with abundance and prosperity. Get ready to transform your limiting beliefs into empowering ones, and unlock the limitless potential that lies within you.

UNEARTHING YOUR MONEY SCRIPT:
What messages did you receive about money growing up?

Our beliefs about money are often shaped by the messages we receive during our formative years. From our parents, teachers, and society at large, we absorb countless lessons about wealth, success, and abundance—some empowering, others limiting.

Our earliest experiences with money have a profound impact on our financial behavior as adults. Think back to your childhood. Were conversations about money shrouded in secrecy or laced with anxiety? Did you hear messages like "*we can't afford that*" or "*money doesn't grow on trees*"? These seemingly harmless phrases can plant seeds of scarcity that linger into adulthood.

Imagine reflecting on your childhood memories, recalling the words spoken by your parents about money—their fears, their dreams, their struggles. Perhaps you heard phrases like "*Money doesn't grow on trees*" or "*We can't afford that.*" These messages, whether explicit or implicit, shape our perception of money and create the blueprint for our financial reality.

In this section, we embark on a journey of introspection, exploring the messages we internalized about money growing up and how they continue to influence our financial beliefs and behaviors.

ACTION STEP: Journal about your earliest memories of money. What emotions were associated with money? Were there specific events that shaped your beliefs? Identifying these patterns is the first step to rewriting your script.

REWRITING YOUR SCRIPT FOR SUCCESS:
Crafting empowering beliefs about Wealth

Armed with awareness, we now have the power to rewrite our money script—to replace limiting beliefs with empowering ones that support our journey to wealth and success. In this section, we dive deep into the process of reframing our beliefs about money, challenging old narratives, and crafting new ones rooted in abundance and possibility.

Picture yourself sitting down with a pen and paper, as you begin to write your own story of financial success. Instead of *"I'll never be able to afford that,"* you write, *"I am capable of creating wealth and abundance in my life."* Instead of *"Money is scarce and hard to come by,"* you affirm, *"Money flows to me easily and effortlessly.*" With each word, you rewrite your script for success, reclaiming your power to shape your financial destiny.

Now that you've unearthed your money story, it's time to rewrite it! Here are some empowering beliefs to replace those limiting ones:

- **Abundance Belief:** Replace "*there's never enough*" with "*prosperity is available to me.*"
- **Deserving Belief:** Challenge the idea that "*wealth is only for the lucky few*" with "*I am worthy of financial abundance.*"
- **Empowerment Belief:** Shift "*money controls me*" to "*I am in control of my finances.*"

ACTION STEP: Create a list of these empowering beliefs and repeat them like affirmations each day. Post them on your bathroom mirror or set them as phone reminders. The constant repetition will reprogram your subconscious mind for success.

BUILDING CONFIDENCE:

Why believing you can achieve Wealth matters

Without belief in our ability to achieve financial success, even the most well-laid plans will falter. In this section, we explore the importance of building confidence in our financial abilities, cultivating a mindset of possibility, and embracing the belief that wealth is within our reach.

Envision yourself standing tall, with a newfound sense of confidence radiating from within. You trust in your ability to overcome obstacles, seize opportunities, and create the life of abundance you desire. With each step forward, your confidence grows stronger, propelling you towards your financial goals with unwavering determination.

Confidence is the fuel that propels you on your wealth-building journey. When you believe you can achieve financial freedom, you're more likely to take action, overcome obstacles, and persevere through challenges. Conversely, a lack of confidence can lead to procrastination, self-doubt, and ultimately, stagnation.

ACTION STEP: Focus on your strengths and accomplishments. Did you manage to pay down a credit card? Did you learn a new skill that could increase your earning potential? Celebrate these victories, no matter how small. Building confidence is a step-by-step process, and acknowledging your progress is key.

Remember, rewriting your money story is an ongoing process. There will be setbacks and moments of doubt. But by consistently challenging your limiting beliefs and replacing them with empowering ones, you'll cultivate the unshakeable confidence needed to unlock your limitless financial potential. With a powerful new script in hand, you're ready to design a roadmap to your financial dreams.

Our beliefs about money weave a powerful narrative that shapes our reality. By unearthing our money script, rewriting limiting beliefs, and building confidence in our financial abilities, we pave the way for a future filled with abundance and prosperity. As we continue on this journey of self-discovery and transformation, remember that the power to create the life of your dreams lies within you.

In the battle against limiting beliefs, knowledge is our greatest weapon, and belief busters are our allies on the journey to financial freedom. By exposing the myths that hold us back and embracing the truth of our limitless potential, we can dismantle the Money Monster and unleash the power of belief to create the life of abundance and prosperity we deserve. As we embark on this journey of transformation, remember that the only limits that exist are the ones we impose on ourselves. It's time to break free from the chains of limitation and embrace the boundless possibilities that await us on the path to wealth and success.

PART 2:

CULTIVATING WEALTH-BUILDING HABITS

~ Chapter 3 ~

THE FOUNDATION:
Cultivating a Wealth Mindset

Cultivating a wealth mindset is the foundational step towards achieving financial success and abundance. It involves a deliberate shift in perspective, beliefs, and behaviors that empower individuals to unlock their full potential and create wealth. Within this foundation, three key components play a pivotal role: Unleashing Your Potential, Overcoming Limiting Beliefs, and Embracing Abundance Thinking.

UNLEASHING YOUR POTENTIAL

Unleashing your potential is about recognizing and harnessing the innate abilities and talents that lie within you. Each individual possesses unique strengths, skills, and passions that, when fully utilized, can propel them towards success in various aspects of life, including finances.

- **Self-discovery and Personal Development**

    The journey towards unleashing your potential begins with self-discovery and personal development. This involves introspection, reflection, and exploration of your interests, values, and aspirations. By gaining clarity on who you are and what you want to achieve, you can align your actions with your authentic self and tap into your inherent potential.

- **Setting Ambitious Goals**

    Setting ambitious yet achievable goals is another crucial aspect of unleashing your potential. Goals provide direction, motivation, and a sense of purpose, guiding your actions towards meaningful outcomes. Whether it's financial independence, entrepreneurship, or career advancement, setting clear and specific goals allows you to channel your energy and resources effectively towards realizing your dreams.

- **Taking Action and Embracing Growth**

Unleashing your potential requires taking bold and decisive action towards your goals. It's about stepping outside your comfort zone, embracing challenges, and continuously pushing the boundaries of what you believe is possible. Through perseverance, resilience, and a commitment to lifelong learning, you can unlock new levels of achievement and fulfillment in your personal and financial endeavors.

OVERCOMING LIMITING BELIEFS

Limiting beliefs are negative thoughts and assumptions that hold you back from reaching your full potential. They often stem from past experiences, societal conditioning, or fear of failure, and can sabotage your efforts to build wealth and achieve success. Overcoming limiting beliefs is essential for cultivating a wealth mindset and unlocking your true potential.

- **Identifying & Challenging Belief Patterns**

The first step in overcoming limiting beliefs is to identify and challenge the belief patterns that are holding you back. This requires introspection and self-awareness to recognize the negative thoughts and self-talk that undermine your confidence and resilience. By questioning the validity of these beliefs and reframing them in a more empowering light, you can break free from their grip and open yourself up to new possibilities.

- **Cultivating a growth mindset**

Cultivating a growth mindset is a powerful antidote to limiting beliefs. Unlike a fixed mindset that views abilities as static and immutable, a growth mindset embraces the belief that intelligence and talent can be developed through effort and perseverance. By adopting a growth mindset, you can overcome self-doubt and fear of failure, embrace challenges as opportunities for growth, and cultivate resilience in the face of setbacks.

- ***Rewriting your inner narrative***

    Rewriting your inner narrative is a transformative process that involves replacing limiting beliefs with empowering affirmations and positive self-talk. Instead of dwelling on past failures or perceived shortcomings, focus on your strengths, achievements, and potential for growth. By consciously reshaping your internal dialogue, you can reprogram your subconscious mind for success and create a more supportive mental environment conducive to wealth creation.

EMBRACING ABUNDANCE THINKING

Abundance thinking is a mindset that acknowledges the infinite possibilities and resources available to us in the world. It is rooted in the belief that there is more than enough to go around and that success is not a zero-sum game. By embracing abundance thinking, you can shift from a scarcity mindset focused on lack and limitation to an abundance mindset characterized by gratitude, generosity, and prosperity.

- **Gratitude and Appreciation**

Gratitude is the cornerstone of abundance thinking. By cultivating a deep sense of gratitude for the blessings and opportunities in your life, you shift your focus from what you lack to what you have. This attitude of appreciation opens your heart and mind to the abundance that surrounds you, fostering a sense of abundance consciousness and attracting more blessings into your life.

- **Visualization and Manifestation**

Visualization and manifestation techniques are powerful tools for cultivating abundance thinking and aligning your thoughts with your desires by vividly imagining your goals and aspirations as already accomplished, you create a mental blueprint that primes your subconscious mind for success. Through consistent visualization and positive affirmations, you can program your mind to attract opportunities, resources, and experiences that support your financial goals.

- **Collaboration and Contribution**

Embracing abundance thinking also involves recognizing the interconnectedness of all beings and the power of collaboration and contribution. Instead of competing for scarce resources, seek to collaborate with others and create win-win partnerships that benefit everyone involved. By sharing your knowledge, skills, and resources with others, you contribute to the collective wealth and prosperity of society while also enriching your own life in the process.

Cultivating a wealth mindset is a transformative journey that involves unleashing your potential, overcoming limiting beliefs, and embracing abundance thinking. By adopting these principles and practices, you can unlock new levels of success, fulfillment, and prosperity in your personal and financial life.

~Chapter 4~

GOAL SETTING:
Crafting a Vision for Financial Success

Goal setting is a fundamental aspect of achieving financial success. It provides direction, clarity, and motivation, guiding individuals towards their desired outcomes and helping them stay focused and accountable along the way. In this chapter, we will explore two key components of goal setting: Setting SMART Goals and Creating Your Wealth Blueprint.

Set SMART Goals

SMART is an acronym that stands for Specific, Measurable, Achievable, Relevant, and Time-bound. By following these criteria, individuals can create goals that are clear, actionable, and attainable, increasing their likelihood of success.

- **Specific**

    Specific goals are clear and well-defined, leaving no room for ambiguity or confusion. Rather than setting vague objectives like "save money" or "earn more," strive to articulate your goals in precise terms. For example, instead of saying "save money," you might set a specific goal to "save $10,000 for a down payment on a house within the next two years.

- **Measurable**

    Measurable goals are quantifiable, allowing you to track your progress and evaluate your performance objectively. Include specific metrics or milestones that will indicate whether you are on track to achieve your goal. For instance, if your goal is to increase your income, you might set a measurable target to "earn an additional $500 per month through freelance work or side hustles."

- **Achievable**

    Achievable goals are realistic and within your reach given your current resources, skills, and circumstances. While it's important to set ambitious goals that stretch your abilities, be mindful of setting yourself up for failure by setting goals that are too far-fetched or unrealistic. Assess your capabilities and constraints realistically, and set goals that you believe you can accomplish with effort and determination.

- **Relevant**

    Relevant goals are aligned with your values, priorities, and long-term objectives. Before setting a goal, consider whether it truly matters to you and whether it contributes to your overall vision for financial success and fulfillment. Avoid pursuing goals simply because they seem impressive or trendy; instead, focus on goals that resonate with your personal aspirations and contribute to your sense of purpose and meaning.

- **Time-Bound**

    Time-bound goals have a clear deadline or timeframe for completion, providing a sense of urgency and accountability. Set specific dates or milestones by which you aim to achieve your goals, breaking down larger objectives into smaller, manageable tasks with deadlines. This helps prevent procrastination and ensures that you stay focused and disciplined in pursuing your goals.

CREATE YOUR WEALTH BLUEPRINT

Creating your wealth blueprint involves developing a strategic plan or roadmap that outlines your financial goals, priorities, and action steps for achieving them. It serves as a guiding framework that helps you make informed decisions, allocate resources effectively, and stay on course towards financial success. Here are some steps you need to take to create your wealth blueprint:

- **Define Your Financial Goal**

  The first step in creating your wealth blueprint is to define your financial goals clearly and specifically. Consider both short-term and long-term objectives, such as saving for retirement, buying a home, paying off debt, or starting a business. Be as detailed as possible, including specific timelines, target amounts, and key milestones for each goal.

- **Assess Your Current Financial Situation**

  Before you can chart a course towards your financial goals, it's essential to assess your current financial situation honestly. Take stock of your income, expenses, assets, and liabilities, as well as any existing savings or investments. Identify areas of strength and areas for improvement, such as reducing unnecessary expenses, increasing your income, or paying down debt.

- **Develop a Strategic Plan**

    Based on your financial goals and current situation, develop a strategic plan that outlines the steps you need to take to achieve your objectives. Break down each goal into actionable tasks, identifying the specific actions, resources, and timelines required for implementation. Consider factors such as budgeting, saving, investing, and income generation strategies, tailoring your plan to your unique circumstances and priorities.

- **Monitor Progress and Adjust as Needed**

    Once you've implemented your wealth blueprint, it's essential to monitor your progress regularly and make adjustments as needed. Track your income, expenses, savings, and investment performance to ensure that you're staying on track towards your goals. Be flexible and adaptive, willing to revise your plan or pivot your approach in response to changing circumstances or new opportunities that arise.

- ***Seek Support and Accountability***

    Finally, don't hesitate to seek support and accountability from trusted advisors, mentors, or financial professionals. Surround yourself with individuals who share your vision for financial success and can offer guidance, encouragement, and constructive feedback along the way. Consider joining networking groups, mastermind sessions, or online communities where you can connect with like-minded individuals and share ideas and experiences.

    In summary, goal setting and creating a wealth blueprint are essential components of achieving financial success. By setting SMART goals and developing a strategic plan for your finances, you can clarify your objectives, stay focused and disciplined, and take proactive steps towards building the future you desire.

~Chapter 5~

WEALTH BUILDING STRATEGIES:
Practical Approaches for Financial Growth

Wealth building strategies encompass a wide range of approaches and tactics aimed at generating and preserving financial assets over time. In this chapter, we will explore three practical and effective strategies you can adopt for financial growth, they include: Investing Wisely, Entrepreneurship and Innovation, and Leveraging Passive Income Streams.

INVEST WISELY:
Stocks, Real-Estate and Beyond

Investing wisely is one of the most time-tested and proven methods for building wealth over the long term. By putting your money to work in various asset classes, you have the potential to generate significant returns and grow your net worth steadily over time. Some key investment avenues include:

- **Stocks**

    Investing in stocks offers the opportunity to own a stake in publicly traded companies and participate in their growth and profitability. Stocks have historically provided attractive returns over the long term, outperforming many other asset classes. By diversifying your stock portfolio across different sectors and industries, you can mitigate risk and capture upside potential.

- **Real Estate**

    Real estate investment involves purchasing, owning, and managing properties with the aim of generating rental income and capital appreciation. Real estate offers several advantages, including the potential for passive income, tax benefits, and inflation hedging. Whether through rental properties, real estate investment trusts (REITs), or real estate crowdfunding platforms, investing in real estate can be a lucrative wealth-building strategy.

- **Beyond Traditional Assets**

In addition to stocks and real estate, there are numerous other investment opportunities available to you as a savvy investor. These may include bonds, mutual funds, exchange-traded funds (ETFs), commodities, cryptocurrencies, and alternative investments such as private equity and venture capital. Diversifying your investment portfolio across different asset classes can help spread risk and optimize returns.

- **Entrepreneurship and Innovation**

Entrepreneurship and innovation are powerful drivers of wealth creation, offering the potential for unlimited upside and financial independence. By starting and growing a successful business or introducing disruptive products or services to the market, you can create value, generate revenue, and build wealth over time. Key principles of entrepreneurship and innovation include:

- **Identify Opportunities**

    To be a successful entrepreneur, you need to have a keen ability to identify unmet needs, market gaps, or emerging trends and capitalize on them with innovative solutions. By staying attuned to changing consumer preferences, technological advancements, and industry dynamics, you can uncover lucrative opportunities for business growth and expansion.

- **Take Calculated Risk**

    Entrepreneurship inherently involves risk-taking, but successful entrepreneurs understand the importance of taking calculated risks. This means if you plan to invest in any business venture, you need to carefully assess the potential rewards and pitfalls of that business venture, conduct thorough market research, and develop a strategic plan to mitigate risks and maximize chances of success.

- **_Continuous Learning & Adaptation_**

The entrepreneurial journey is characterized by constant learning, experimentation, and adaptation. To be a successful entrepreneur, you have to embrace a growth mindset and remain open to feedback, criticism, and new ideas. You also have to be willing to pivot your business strategies, iterate on your products or services, and evolve with changing market conditions to stay competitive and resilient.

LEVERAGE PASSIVE INCOME STREAMS

Passive income streams are sources of income that require minimal ongoing effort or active involvement to maintain. By generating passive income, you can create financial stability, supplement your earned income, and ultimately achieve financial freedom. Some common passive income streams include:

- **Rental Income**

Owning rental properties and collecting rental income from tenants is a classic example of passive income generation. While managing rental properties may require some initial effort in terms of property acquisition, tenant screening, and maintenance, rental income can provide a steady and reliable source of cash flow over time.

- **Dividend Income**

Investing in dividend-paying stocks or dividend-focused mutual funds allows investors to earn regular dividend income without having to sell their shares. Dividend income is typically distributed quarterly or annually by companies to their shareholders as a reward for owning their stock. By reinvesting dividends or relying on them for living expenses, investors can create a passive income stream from their investments.

- **Royalties and Licensing Fees**

If you are a creator, author, an artist, or an inventor, you can generate passive income by licensing your intellectual property or creative works to third parties in exchange for royalties or licensing fees. This may include royalties from book sales, licensing fees for patents or trademarks, or royalties from music or film royalties.

- **Affiliate Marketing & Passive Income**

Affiliate marketing involves promoting third-party products or services and earning a commission for each sale or referral generated through your affiliate links. Similarly, creating passive income streams through online businesses, digital products, or membership sites can provide recurring revenue with minimal ongoing effort.

Wealth building strategies encompass a diverse array of approaches for generating and preserving financial assets. By investing wisely, embracing entrepreneurship and innovation, and leveraging passive income streams, you can take proactive steps towards achieving your financial goals and building lasting wealth for yourself and future generations.

~Chapter 6~

FROM SPENDER TO SAVER:
Mastering the Art of Financial Discipline

In the pursuit of financial freedom, one of the most critical transitions one must make is from a spender to a saver. This shift in mindset and behavior is fundamental to building wealth and securing a stable financial future.

The path to financial freedom is paved with good habits. Just like building a strong physique requires consistent exercise, achieving financial security demands discipline with your money. In this chapter, we delve into the art of financial discipline, exploring budgeting basics, the power of saying "no" to impulse purchases, and the importance of adopting a "pay yourself first" mentality. We'll transform you from a carefree spender into a mindful saver, taking control of your cash flow and building a solid foundation for your financial future.

BUDGETING BASICS:
Taking Control of Your Cash Flow

At the heart of financial discipline lies the practice of budgeting—a fundamental tool for managing your money and taking control of your cash flow. A budget serves as a roadmap for your finances, helping you allocate your income towards essential expenses, savings, debt repayment, and discretionary spending. By tracking your income and expenses, you gain clarity and insight into your financial habits and can make informed decisions to align your spending with your financial goals.

Consider the story of Emily, a recent college graduate who struggled with overspending and debt until she implemented a budgeting system. By creating a monthly budget that outlined her income, expenses, and savings goals, Emily gained a newfound sense of control over her finances. With a clear understanding of where her money was going, Emily was able to prioritize her spending, pay off her debt, and start building wealth for the future.

Imagine your income as a flowing river, without a proper irrigation system, this precious resource will simply run off, leaving your financial fields parched. Budgeting is your irrigation system, ensuring every dollar is channeled towards your financial goals. Here's how to create a budget that works for you:

- **Track Your Income:** List all your income sources – salary, side hustles, rental income, etc. Be honest and realistic about your average monthly income.
- **Track Your Expenses:** For a month, meticulously track every penny you spend – groceries, rent, entertainment, everything.

Categorize your expenses (essentials, discretionary spending, debt payments).
- **Analyze Your Spending:** Once you have a month's worth of data, analyze your spending habits. Are there areas where you can cut back? Are there unnecessary subscriptions draining your finances?
- **Create a Spending Plan:** Allocate your income towards different categories. Essentials like rent and groceries come first. Then, factor in savings and debt repayment goals. Leave a reasonable amount for discretionary spending (entertainment, dining out).

Illustration: Let's say your monthly income is $4,000. Essentials like rent, utilities, and groceries cost $2,000. You allocate $500 for debt repayment and $200 for savings. This leaves you with $1,300 for discretionary spending. You can further break this down into categories like dining out, entertainment, and clothes.

THE POWER OF "NO":
Prioritizing saving and Investing over Impulse Purchases

In a world of instant gratification and consumerism, learning to say "no" to impulse purchases is essential for financial discipline. While it can be tempting to indulge in spontaneous spending, particularly in the age of online shopping and easy credit, such purchases often derail your financial goals and undermine your long-term financial security. By prioritizing saving and investing over impulse purchases, you set yourself on the path to building wealth and achieving financial freedom.

Imagine walking into a store and encountering a tempting display of the latest gadgets or designer clothing. Instead of giving in to the urge to splurge, pause and ask yourself whether the purchase aligns with your financial goals and priorities. By practicing self-control and delaying gratification, you empower yourself to make intentional financial decisions that support your long-term financial well-being.

We've all been there – the enticing online sale, the trendy new gadget everyone's talking about. Impulse purchases can derail your financial plans. Learning to say "no" to these temptations is a crucial step towards becoming a master saver.

ACTION STEP: Employ the "24-Hour Rule" before making any non-essential purchase. Wait 24 hours before buying something. Often, the initial desire fades, and you realize you don't truly need the item.

BUILDING A "PAY YOURSELF FIRST" MENTALITY

One of the most powerful habits you can cultivate on your journey to financial freedom is the "*pay yourself first*" mentality. This principle entails prioritizing savings and investments by setting aside a portion of your income before paying for expenses or discretionary spending. By treating savings as a non-negotiable expense, you ensure that your financial future takes precedence over immediate wants and desires.

Consider the story of James, who automated his savings by setting up automatic transfers from his checking account to his savings and investment accounts each month. By paying himself first, James made saving a priority and consistently contributed towards his long-term financial goals. Over time, his savings grew, and he was able to build a nest egg that provided financial security and peace of mind.

Traditionally, we pay our bills and then save what's leftover. But what if we flipped the script? The "*Pay Yourself First*" mentality prioritizes saving and investing. Here's how it works:

- **Automate Your Savings:** Set up an automatic transfer from your checking account to your savings account as soon as you get paid. This "set it and forget it" approach ensures you save consistently.
- **Think of Savings as a Bill:** Treat your savings goals like a fixed monthly expense. This shift in mindset makes saving feel less like a burden and more like a necessary step towards your financial future.

By implementing these strategies, you'll transform from a reactive spender to a proactive saver. Remember, financial discipline is a muscle that gets stronger with consistent exercise. The more you practice these habits, the easier it will become to control your cash flow and prioritize your financial goals.

In the journey to financial freedom, mastering the art of financial discipline is essential. By adopting budgeting basics, prioritizing saving and investing over impulse purchases, and embracing a "pay yourself first" mentality, you lay the foundation for building wealth and achieving your financial goals. As you cultivate these wealth-building habits, remember that small changes today can lead to significant financial rewards tomorrow. In the next chapter, we'll explore powerful strategies to not only save but also grow your wealth through smart investing.

~Chapter 7~

THE COMPOUND EFFECT:
How Small Habits Lead to Big Riches

In the realm of wealth creation, the concept of the compound effect reigns supreme - a seemingly simple principle with profound implications for our financial future. In this chapter, we delve into the transformative power of small habits, exploring how the seed of wealth, daily money wins, and the transformation of the "latte factor" can lead to monumental riches beyond our wildest dreams.

Imagine planting a tiny seed in fertile soil. With consistent care – watering, sunlight, nourishment – that seed transforms into a mighty oak, a testament to the power of growth over time. The same principle applies to your finances. Small, consistent efforts fueled by the *compound effect* can blossom into significant wealth over the long term.

Picture yourself starting a retirement account in your 20s, contributing a small amount each month. As the years pass, your contributions earn interest, which in turn earns interest on itself, creating a snowball effect that accelerates your wealth accumulation. By harnessing the power of compound interest, you set yourself on the path to financial independence and abundance.

THE SEED OF WEALTH:

Understanding the power of Compound Interest

Compound interest is often referred to as the "eighth wonder of the world" by Albert Einstein, and for good reason. It's the magic that allows your money to grow exponentially. Here's how it works:

- ***Interest on Interest:*** Compound interest means you earn interest not just on your initial investment but also on the accumulated interest from previous periods. It's like a snowball rolling downhill, gathering momentum as it goes.

Illustration: Let's say you invest $1,000 at an annual interest rate of 5%. In one year, you'll earn $50 in interest, bringing your total to $1,050. In the second year, you'll not only earn interest on the initial $1,000 but also on the $50 you earned earlier. This translates to $52.50 in interest, bringing your total to $1,102.50. See how the interest amount keeps growing over time? That's the power of compound interest!

DAILY MONEY WINS:
Small habits that create lasting change

While the allure of overnight success may captivate our imagination, the reality is that lasting wealth is built one small habit at a time.

In this section, we explore the concept of daily money wins—simple, actionable habits that, when practiced consistently, lead to significant financial gains over time.

Consider the story of Lisa, who made a commitment to track her spending daily and allocate a portion of her income towards savings and investments. By making small adjustments to her daily habits, such as bringing lunch from home instead of eating out or opting for a bike ride instead of a costly gym membership, Lisa was able to free up extra cash to put towards her financial goals. Over time, these small changes compounded into substantial savings and investments, laying the foundation for a secure financial future.

The beauty of the compound effect is that it doesn't require massive investments. Even small, consistent contributions can lead to impressive results over time. Here are some "daily money wins" that leverage the compound effect:

- **Automate Savings:** Set up an automatic transfer of even a small amount (say, $25) from your checking to your savings account every payday. Over time, this can add up significantly.
- **Embrace the "Latte Factor":** Skip that daily $5 latte and invest the money instead. Invested consistently over 20 years with a 7% annual return, that $5 could grow to over $20,000!
- **Challenge Yourself with Savings Games:** Try the "52-Week Challenge" where you save a progressively larger amount each week (week 1: $1, week 2: $2, etc.). By the end of the year, you'll have saved over $1,300.

FROM LATTE FACTOR TO MILLIONAIRE MAKER:
Making every Penny count

The "latte factor" is a term coined to describe the seemingly insignificant daily expenses—such as a daily coffee or a takeout meal—that, over time, can add up to significant amounts of money. In this section, we challenge the notion that small expenses are inconsequential and instead illustrate how making every penny count can be the difference between financial mediocrity and wealth.

Imagine redirecting the money you would spend on daily indulgences towards investments that generate passive income and wealth. By cutting back on discretionary spending and prioritizing savings and investments, you transform the "latte factor" from a drain on your finances to a millionaire maker—a powerful tool for building lasting wealth and financial freedom.

The "latte factor" might seem insignificant, but it's a powerful illustration of how seemingly small choices can have a major impact on your financial future. Here's the key:

- **Every penny count:** Don't underestimate the power of small, consistent savings.
- **Start Early:** The earlier you start investing, the more time your money has to benefit from compound interest.
- **Develop a "Growth Mindset":** Believe in the power of your small actions to create big results.

By embracing these principles, you'll transform from a passive observer to an active participant in your financial future. Remember, the compound effect is a marathon, not a sprint. The key is to start early, stay consistent, and watch your wealth grow steadily over time. In the next chapter, we'll delve into the exciting world of investing, equipping you with the knowledge and tools to make your money work for you.

In the journey to financial independence, the compound effect is our greatest ally—a force that transforms small habits into monumental riches over time. By understanding the power of compound interest, embracing daily money wins, and making every penny count, we unlock the door to a future filled with abundance and prosperity. As we continue on this journey of wealth creation, remember that every action, no matter how small, has the potential to shape our financial destiny. It's time to harness the power of the compound effect and pave the way for a brighter, wealthier future.

PART 3:

EMBRACING ABUNDANCE

~Chapter 8~

MINDFULNESS AND MONEY:
Developing a Healthy Relationship with Wealth

Mindfulness and money are two concepts that may seem unrelated at first glance, but they are deeply intertwined in our lives and can profoundly influence our relationship with wealth and financial well-being. Developing a healthy relationship with wealth involves cultivating mindfulness—a state of present-moment awareness and non-judgmental acceptance—as well as adopting practices that promote gratitude, conscious money management, and balance between material wealth and overall well-being.

WEALTH IS A MINDSET, NOT A NUMBER:

So far, we've explored strategies to build wealth and cultivate financial discipline. But financial freedom is more than just accumulating a certain number in your bank account. It's about achieving a sense of *wholeness and fulfillment* that allows you to live life on your own terms.

In the journey to financial freedom, it's easy to get caught up in the pursuit of numbers—bank account balances, investment portfolios, net worth figures. But true wealth transcends mere digits on a screen; it is a state of mind, a mindset that shapes our perception of success and abundance. In this chapter, we will explore the profound truth that wealth is a mindset, not a number, and learn how to redefine success on our own terms. We'll redefine success by shifting the focus from just the bottom line to a holistic view of abundance.

BEYOND THE BOTTOM LINE:

While financial success is undeniably important, it is not the sole measure of a fulfilling life. True wealth encompasses far more than monetary riches; it includes health, relationships, personal growth, and contribution to society. By expanding our definition of success beyond the bottom line, we open ourselves up to a wealth of opportunities for fulfillment and happiness.

Consider the story of John, a successful entrepreneur who built a multimillion-dollar business but sacrificed his health, relationships, and happiness in the process. Despite his financial success, John found himself feeling empty and unfulfilled, realizing that true wealth cannot be measured solely in dollars and cents. Through introspection and reflection, John redefined success on his own terms, prioritizing balance, well-being, and purpose in his life. By embracing a holistic approach to wealth, John discovered a newfound sense of fulfillment and abundance that transcended monetary riches.

Financial freedom isn't a one-size-fits-all proposition. For some, it might mean early retirement and traveling the world. For others, it might be the freedom to pursue a creative passion or spend more time with loved ones. The key is to *define success on your own terms*.

ACTION STEP: Journal about your ideal life. What would a truly fulfilling day look like for you? What experiences or goals would bring you joy and a sense of accomplishment? Visualize this ideal life and use it as your guiding light on your financial freedom journey.

GRATITUDE IS THE GATEWAY TO ABUNDANCE

Gratitude is the practice of acknowledging and appreciating the blessings, opportunities, and abundance in our lives. When it comes to money, cultivating gratitude involves shifting our focus from what we lack to what we have and recognizing the positive aspects of our financial situation.

Gratitude is a powerful force that has the ability to transform our perception of abundance and attract more of what we appreciate into our lives. When we cultivate an appreciation mindset, we shift our focus from scarcity to abundance, from what we lack to what we have. By acknowledging and expressing gratitude for the blessings, opportunities, and abundance in our lives, we open ourselves up to receive even more blessings and abundance in return.

Imagine waking up each day with a sense of gratitude for the simple joys of life—the warmth of the sun on your face, the laughter of loved ones, the beauty of nature. By practicing gratitude daily through journaling, meditation, or simply pausing to appreciate the present moment, we cultivate an appreciation mindset that infuses every aspect of our lives with richness and abundance.

Gratitude isn't just a feel-good emotion; it's a powerful tool for attracting abundance. When you focus on what you already have, you open yourself up to receiving more.

ACTION STEP: Start a gratitude practice. Every day, list five things you're grateful for, big or small. This could be anything from your health and loved ones to a delicious cup of coffee. By expressing gratitude, you shift your mindset from scarcity to abundance.

Here are some ways to cultivate gratitude in relation to money:

- **Counting your Blessings:** Take time each day to reflect on the things you are grateful for in your financial life. This could include having a stable income, a roof over your head, food on the table, supportive friends and family, or opportunities for financial growth. By consciously acknowledging and appreciating these blessings, you cultivate a sense of abundance and contentment.

- **Keeping a Gratitude Journal:** Consider keeping a gratitude journal where you regularly write down things you are grateful for, including financial blessings, opportunities, and acts of kindness you've received. Reflecting on these moments of gratitude can help shift your perspective from scarcity to abundance and cultivate a positive mindset towards money and wealth.
- **Practicing Generosity:** Another way to cultivate gratitude is by practicing generosity and giving back to others. Whether through charitable donations, volunteering your time and skills, or supporting causes you believe in, acts of generosity remind us of the abundance we have and the impact we can make in the lives of others. By giving freely without

expecting anything in return, we cultivate a sense of gratitude and interconnectedness with the world around us.

HOW GENEROSITY CREATES PROSPERITY

Contrary to popular belief, generosity is not a zero-sum game; it is a powerful catalyst for creating prosperity and abundance for both the giver and the receiver. When we give freely of our time, resources, and talents, we not only enrich the lives of others but also experience a profound sense of fulfillment and purpose.

Consider the story of Sarah, a successful executive who devoted her time and resources to charitable causes and community service. Despite her demanding career and busy schedule, Sarah found immense joy and satisfaction in giving back to others. Through her generosity, Sarah not only made a positive impact on the lives of those in need but also cultivated a sense of abundance and prosperity in her own life.

The paradox of abundance is that true wealth comes not just from accumulating but also from giving. When you share your resources with others, you create a ripple effect of generosity that ultimately flows back to you.

ACTION STEP: Incorporate giving into your financial plan. Volunteer your time, donate to a cause you care about, or simply mentor someone in need. Acts of generosity not only benefit others but also cultivate a sense of abundance and purpose in your own life.

Remember, financial freedom is a journey, not a destination.

It's about cultivating a mindset of abundance, appreciating what you have, and using your resources to create a life filled with meaning and fulfillment. By embracing these principles, you'll not only achieve financial security but also unlock a wealth of happiness and well-being in all aspects of your life. The road ahead may have its challenges, but with the right mindset and the tools you've gained throughout this guide, you're well-equipped to navigate them and claim your own definition of financial freedom!

In the pursuit of financial freedom, it is essential to remember that wealth is not merely a number; it is a mindset—a mindset that embraces abundance, gratitude, and generosity. By redefining success on our own terms, cultivating an appreciation mindset, and giving back to others, we open ourselves up to a world of abundance and prosperity beyond measure. As we embrace the principles of abundance in our lives, we unlock the true essence of wealth and create a future filled with fulfillment, joy, and abundance.

MANAGING MONEY MINDFULLY

Managing money mindfully involves bringing awareness and intentionality to your financial decisions and behaviors. It means being fully present and conscious of your spending, saving, and investing habits, as well as the emotions and beliefs that influence our relationship with money. Here are some principles of mindful money management:

- **Budgeting and Spending Consciously:** Create a budget that aligns with your financial goals, values, and priorities, and track your expenses mindfully to ensure you're spending money intentionally and in line with your values. Before making a purchase, pause and ask yourself whether it aligns with your needs and values, or if it's driven by impulse or emotional spending.
- **Practicing Delayed Gratification:** Mindful money management involves practicing delayed gratification and resisting the urge

for immediate rewards or instant gratification. Instead of giving in to impulse purchases or lifestyle inflation, consider delaying purchases and saving towards meaningful goals that align with your long-term aspirations. By prioritizing delayed gratification, you cultivate discipline and resilience in managing your finances.

- **Mindful Investing:** Approach investing with mindfulness by conducting thorough research, assessing risk factors, and aligning your investment choices with your financial goals and risk tolerance. Avoid making impulsive investment decisions driven by fear or greed, and instead, focus on building a diversified investment portfolio that reflects your values and long-term objectives.

BALANCING WEALTH AND WELL-BEING

Balancing wealth and well-being involve recognizing that true prosperity encompasses more than just financial wealth—it also includes physical health, emotional well-being, relationships, and personal fulfillment. Here are some strategies for achieving balance between wealth and well-being:

- ***Prioritizing Self-care:*** Invest in your physical, emotional, and mental well-being by prioritizing self-care practices such as exercise, healthy eating, meditation, and relaxation techniques. Taking care of your overall well-being not only enhances your quality of life but also improves your ability to manage stress and make sound financial decisions.

- ***Cultivating Meaningful Relationships:*** Nurture your relationships with family, friends, and community, as they are essential sources of support, connection, and happiness. Spend quality time with loved ones, engage in meaningful conversations, and offer support and encouragement to those in need. Strong social connections contribute to a sense of belonging and fulfillment that goes beyond material wealth.

- **Pursuing Fulfilling Activities:** Engage in activities and pursuits that bring you joy, fulfillment, and a sense of purpose outside of work and financial endeavors. Whether it's pursuing hobbies, volunteering, or pursuing personal interests and passions, allocating time and resources to activities that nourish your soul and bring meaning to your life is essential for holistic well-being.

~Chapter 9~

TAMING THE FEAR FACTOR:
Making Smart Investment Decisions

Congratulations! You've conquered your limiting beliefs, mastered the art of saving, and embraced the true essence of abundance. Now it's time to unleash the power of your hard-earned money and put it to work for you – through the exciting world of investing! But before you dive headfirst into the stock market, let's address the elephant in the room: FEAR.

Investing can be a thrilling adventure, but it's often fraught with fear and uncertainty. In this chapter, we'll explore how to tame the fear factor, make smart investment decisions, and navigate the complex world of finance with confidence and clarity.

Investing can be intimidating, conjuring images of volatile markets and potential losses. But fear not, intrepid adventurer! This chapter equips you with the knowledge and tools to navigate the investment landscape with confidence, making smart decisions aligned with your risk tolerance and long-term goals.

UNDERSTANDING RISK TOLERANCE:
Finding the investment strategy right for you

Risk tolerance is a crucial aspect of investing that often gets overlooked. It's the measure of how much uncertainty you can handle in your investment portfolio. In this section, we delve into the different types of risk, from market volatility to inflation, and help you assess your own risk tolerance.

Imagine yourself on a roller coaster. Some people love the exhilarating twists and turns, while others feel nauseous at the mere thought. Your risk tolerance is like your tolerance for roller coasters—some investors thrive on the excitement of high-risk investments, while others prefer a smoother ride with lower-risk options. By understanding your risk tolerance, you can tailor your investment strategy to suit your individual preferences and goals.

Risk and return are two sides of the investment coin. Higher potential returns often come with greater risk of loss. The key is to *find the investment sweet spot* that aligns with your risk tolerance.

Here's a breakdown of different risk profiles:

- **Conservative Investor:** A conservative investor Prioritizes capital preservation over high returns. Focuses on low-risk investments like bonds and CDs.
- **Moderate Investor:** Seeks a balance between risk and reward. Invests in a mix of stocks, bonds, and other asset classes.

- ***Aggressive Investor:*** Comfortable with higher risk for the potential of higher returns. Invests heavily in stocks and other growth-oriented assets.

    ACTION STEP: Evaluate your risk tolerance. Consider your age, financial goals, and time horizon. Are you saving for retirement in 20 years, or a down payment on a house in 2 years? Your risk tolerance will influence your investment choices.

INVESTING FOR THE LONG TERM:

Avoiding Get-Rich-Quick schemes and Short-Term Thinking

In a world of instant gratification, it's easy to be seduced by get-rich-quick schemes and short-term thinking. But true wealth is built over time through patience, discipline, and a long-term perspective. In this section, we explore the importance of investing for the long term and avoiding the pitfalls of short-sighted decisions.

Think of investing as planting a garden. You wouldn't expect to harvest a bountiful crop overnight—you need to plant the seeds, nurture the soil, and wait patiently for the fruits of your labor to ripen. Similarly, successful investing requires patience, discipline, and a focus on the long term. By resisting the temptation to chase quick profits and instead focusing on building a solid foundation for the future, you set yourself up for lasting financial success.

The allure of get-rich-quick schemes is strong, but the reality of investing is that it's a marathon, not a sprint. Building long-term wealth requires patience, discipline, and a focus on the bigger picture. But here are some few rules to follow:

- **Beware of:** Investment opportunities promising high returns with little risk. These

are often scams designed to separate you from your hard-earned money.
- **Focus on:** Building a diversified portfolio of assets that will grow steadily over time. This approach helps weather market fluctuations and smooths out your investment journey.

BUILDING A DIVERSIFIED PORTFOLIO:
Spreading your Wealth to mitigate Risk

Diversification is the cornerstone of a successful investment strategy. By spreading your wealth across different asset classes, industries, and geographic regions, you can mitigate risk and enhance your chances of long-term growth. In this section, we explore the benefits of diversification and offer practical tips for building a well-balanced investment portfolio.

Imagine you're building a house. You wouldn't put all your eggs in one basket by constructing the entire structure out of fragile glass. Instead, you'd use a mix of materials—brick, wood, steel—to ensure stability and resilience. Similarly, a diversified investment portfolio spreads your risk and protects you from the ups and downs of individual assets or sectors. By diversifying your investments, you can weather market fluctuations with confidence and achieve your financial goals.

Diversification is the investor's golden rule. It means spreading your investments across different asset classes to minimize risk. Here are some key asset classes to consider:

- **Stocks:** Represent ownership in companies and offer the potential for high growth but also carry higher risk.
- **Bonds:** Issued by governments and corporations, offering regular interest payments and considered lower risk than stocks.
- **Real Estate:** Investing in physical property or through Real Estate Investment Trusts

(REITs) can provide steady income and long-term appreciation.
- **Cash and Cash Equivalents:** Low-risk options like savings accounts and money market funds offer liquidity and stability.

ILLUSTRATION: Let's say you're a moderate investor with a 10-year investment horizon. You could allocate your portfolio as follows: 60% stocks (for growth), 30% bonds (for stability), and 10% cash (for emergencies).

By understanding your risk tolerance, adopting a long-term perspective, and building a diversified portfolio, you'll be well-equipped to navigate the investment landscape with confidence. Remember, knowledge is power. The more you educate yourself about investing, the more control you'll have over your financial future. In the next chapter, we'll explore some valuable resources and strategies to help you get started on your investment journey.

In the fast-paced world of investing, taming the fear factor is essential for making smart decisions and building wealth for the future. By understanding your risk tolerance, investing for the long term, and building a diversified portfolio, you can navigate the complexities of the financial markets with confidence and clarity. As you embark on your investment journey, remember that knowledge is your most powerful weapon, and patience is your greatest ally. With the right mindset and strategy, you can tame the fear factor and unlock the door to a future of financial abundance and security.

PART 4:

MAINTAINING THE MOMENTUM

~Chapter 10~

STAYING MOTIVATED:
Overcoming Obstacles and Sticking to Your Plan

In the final leg of our journey to financial freedom, we confront the challenge of staying motivated amidst obstacles and setbacks. This chapter is a testament to the resilience of the human spirit and the power of perseverance in achieving our goals. We'll explore how to overcome doubts, celebrate milestones, and build a support system that propels us forward on our path to success.

The road to financial freedom is paved with good intentions, but even the most well-laid plans can encounter detours. Life throws curveballs, temptations arise, and sometimes, staying motivated can feel like a constant battle. This chapter equips you with the tools to overcome obstacles, silence self-doubt, and maintain the momentum towards your financial goals.

THE POWER OF POSITIVE SELF-TALK:

Our minds can be our greatest allies or our fiercest adversaries on the road to success. In this section, we delve into the power of positive self-talk—the practice of reframing negative thoughts and doubts into empowering beliefs and affirmations.

Imagine you're climbing a steep mountain trail, your legs burning with exertion and doubt creeping into your mind. Instead of succumbing to negative self-talk—telling yourself you're not strong enough or capable enough—you harness the power of positive affirmations. With each step, you repeat phrases like "I am strong," "I am resilient," "I am unstoppable." By shifting your mindset from one of doubt to one of confidence and determination, you propel yourself forward towards your goal.

Our inner voice is a powerful force. Negative thoughts like "I can't do this" or "I'll never be rich" can derail your progress. Here's how to silence the inner critic and harness the power of positive self-talk:

- **Challenge Negative Thoughts:** When a negative thought arises, question its validity. Replace it with a positive affirmation like "I am capable" or "I am worthy of financial abundance."
- **Focus on Progress, Not Perfection:** Don't beat yourself up for occasional slip-ups. Celebrate your small victories, no matter how insignificant they seem. Every step forward takes you closer to your goals.
- **Visualize Success:** Take a few minutes each day to visualize yourself achieving your financial goals. See yourself living

comfortably, debt-free, or pursuing your dreams. This mental rehearsal boosts motivation and reinforces your commitment.

Illustration: Let's say you have a setback – you overspend on an impulse purchase. Instead of spiraling into negativity, acknowledge the slip-up, remind yourself of your long-term goals, and recommit to your plan.

CELEBRATING MILESTONES:

In the pursuit of long-term goals, it's easy to lose sight of the progress we've made along the way. In this section, we emphasize the importance of celebrating milestones—small victories that remind us of how far we've come and inspire us to keep pushing forward.

Think of your financial journey as a marathon, with checkpoints along the way to mark your progress. Whether it's paying off a credit card debt, reaching a savings goal, or achieving a milestone in your investment portfolio, each accomplishment deserves to be celebrated. By acknowledging your achievements and taking time to reflect on your progress, you renew your motivation and fuel your determination to continue on your path to success.

In the journey to financial freedom, it's easy to get discouraged if you only focus on the finish line. Celebrate your milestones along the way to stay inspired:

- **Reaching Savings Goals:** Did you finally hit your emergency fund target? Treat yourself to a small reward to acknowledge your accomplishment.
- **Debt Reduction Milestones:** Every debt you pay off is a victory. Celebrate these milestones, big or small, to stay motivated on your debt-free journey.

- ***Investment Growth:*** Track the progress of your investments. Witnessing your wealth grow, even incrementally, can be a powerful motivator to keep going.

BUILDING A SUPPORT SYSTEM:

No one achieves success alone. In this section, we explore the importance of building a support system—a network of friends, family, mentors, and like-minded individuals who cheer you on, provide guidance, and lift you up when you're feeling down.

Imagine you're part of a team, each member offering encouragement, support, and camaraderie on the journey to victory. Whether it's a financial advisor helping you navigate investment decisions, a friend holding you accountable to your savings goals, or a mentor offering wisdom and guidance, your support system is there to bolster your confidence and keep you motivated when the going gets tough.

Surrounding yourself with positive and like-minded individuals can significantly impact your financial journey. Here's how to build a supportive network:

- **Find an Accountability Partner:** Share your financial goals with a friend or family member who will support and hold you accountable.
- **Join Online Communities:** Connect with others on similar financial journeys through online forums or social media groups. Share experiences, offer encouragement, and learn from each other's successes and challenges.
- **Seek Guidance from a Financial Coach**: Consider working with a financial coach who can provide personalized advice and motivation to stay on track.

Remember, financial freedom is not a solo act.

Having a strong support system can make a world of difference in your journey. By implementing these strategies, you'll cultivate the unwavering self-belief, celebrate your victories, and surround yourself with positive influences – all essential ingredients for maintaining the momentum and achieving your financial dreams.

As we progress on our journey to financial freedom, remember that maintaining momentum is essential for achieving lasting success. By harnessing the power of positive self-talk, celebrating milestones, and building a support system, you can overcome obstacles, stay motivated, and stick to your plan with unwavering determination. As you continue on your path to success, may you find strength in adversity, inspiration in progress, and support in the company of like-minded individuals. With perseverance and resilience, the future is yours to create.

~Chapter 11~

OVERCOMING CHALLENGES:
Resilience in the Face of Adversity

Overcoming challenges and building resilience are essential skills for achieving long-term success, especially in the realm of finances where uncertainty and setbacks are inevitable. In this section, we will explore strategies for developing resilience in the face of adversity, focusing on navigating financial setbacks, overcoming the fear of failure, and building resilience for long-term success.

NAVIGATING FINANCIAL SETBACKS

Financial setbacks are a common part of life and can take many forms, such as job loss, unexpected expenses, market downturns, or business failures. Navigating these setbacks requires resilience, adaptability, and a proactive approach to managing challenges. Here are some strategies for overcoming financial setbacks:

- **Assessing the Situation:** The first step in navigating financial setbacks is to assess the situation calmly and objectively. Take stock of your current financial situation, including your income, expenses, savings, debts, and assets. Identify the root causes of the setback and the potential impact on your financial goals and well-being.
- **Creating a Contingency Plan:** Develop a contingency plan to address the immediate challenges and mitigate the impact of the setback. This may involve cutting expenses, tapping into emergency savings, exploring additional sources of income, negotiating with creditors, or seeking financial assistance or support from friends, family, or community resources.

- ***Learning from the Experience:*** View financial setbacks as learning opportunities rather than failures. Reflect on the lessons learned from the experience, such as identifying areas for improvement in your financial planning, risk management, or emergency preparedness. Use this knowledge to adjust your strategies and behaviors going forward and build resilience against future setbacks.
- ***Maintaining Perspective:*** Maintain perspective and avoid catastrophizing or dwelling on negative outcomes. Remember that setbacks are temporary and can be overcome with time, effort, and perseverance. Focus on what you can control, such as your attitudes, actions, and resilience, rather than fixating on factors beyond your control.

OVERCOMING FEAR OF FAILURE

Fear of failure is a common barrier to success that can prevent individuals from taking risks, pursuing opportunities, or stepping outside their comfort zones. Overcoming this fear requires developing resilience, self-confidence, and a growth mindset. Here are some strategies for overcoming the fear of failure:

- **Embracing Failure as a Learning Opportunity:** Shift your perspective on failure and view it as a natural and necessary part of the learning and growth process. Instead of fearing failure, embrace it as an opportunity to gain valuable insights, develop new skills, and refine your approach. Recognize that failure is not a reflection of your worth or abilities but rather a stepping stone on the path to success.
- **Setting Realistic Expectations:** Set realistic expectations for yourself and acknowledge that success rarely comes without setbacks

or challenges along the way. Avoid perfectionism and the need for validation from others, and focus instead on making progress towards your goals, regardless of the outcome. Celebrate small wins and milestones to boost your confidence and motivation.

- **Cultivating Resilience & Self-compassion:** Build resilience by developing coping mechanisms and strategies for managing stress, setbacks, and disappointments. Practice self-compassion and treat yourself with kindness and understanding, especially during times of failure or adversity. Remember that everyone experiences setbacks and that failure does not define your worth or potential.
- **Taking Calculated Risks:** Take calculated risks and step outside your comfort zone to pursue opportunities for growth and achievement. Recognize that failure is often a byproduct of pushing boundaries and

exploring new possibilities. By taking risks and embracing uncertainty, you expand your comfort zone, build resilience, and increase your chances of success in the long run.

BUILDING RESILIENCE FOR LONG-TERM SUCCESS

Building resilience is essential for achieving long-term success in any endeavor, including finances. Resilience enables individuals to bounce back from setbacks, adapt to change, and thrive in the face of adversity. Here are some strategies for building resilience for long-term success:

- **Cultivating a growth mindset:** Develop a growth mindset that embraces challenges, sees failures as opportunities for growth, and believes in the power of effort and perseverance. Cultivate optimism, resilience, and a belief in your ability to overcome obstacles and achieve your goals, no matter how daunting they may seem.

- ***Developing Coping Skills:*** Develop coping skills and strategies for managing stress, anxiety, and negative emotions effectively. This may include practices such as mindfulness meditation, deep breathing exercises, journaling, or seeking support from friends, family, or mental health professionals. By cultivating healthy coping mechanisms, you build resilience and emotional strength to weather life's challenges.
- ***Building Social Support:*** Build a strong support network of friends, family, mentors, and peers who can offer encouragement, advice, and practical assistance during times of need. Surround yourself with positive influences who uplift and inspire you, and lean on your support network for guidance and support when facing adversity.

- ***Maintaining Flexibility and Adaptability:*** Stay flexible and adaptable in the face of change, uncertainty, and unexpected events. Embrace a mindset of continuous learning and growth, and be willing to adjust your plans, strategies, and expectations as needed to navigate shifting circumstances. By remaining open-minded and adaptable, you can respond effectively to challenges and seize new opportunities for success.

~Chapter 12~

MASTERING THE WEALTH MINDSET:
Tools and Techniques for Lasting Prosperity

Mastering the wealth mindset involves adopting a set of tools and techniques that empower individuals to cultivate abundance, achieve financial goals, and sustain lasting prosperity. In this section, we will explore three key strategies for mastering the wealth mindset: Visualization and Affirmations, Practicing Self-Discipline and Delayed Gratification, and Surrounding Yourself with Success. The final chapter of this guide serves as a treasure chest of valuable tips and reminders to keep you focused and empowered on your path to financial freedom.

VISUALIZATION AND AFFIRMATIONS

Visualization and affirmations are powerful techniques for programming the subconscious mind and aligning your thoughts and beliefs with your financial goals. By vividly imagining your desired outcomes and reinforcing them with positive affirmations, you can cultivate a mindset of abundance and attract wealth into your life. Here's how to harness the power of visualization and affirmations:

- **Visualize your Goals:** Take time each day to visualize your financial goals as if they have already been achieved. Close your eyes and imagine yourself living the life you desire, experiencing the abundance, success, and fulfillment you seek. Visualize the details of your ideal lifestyle, including your home, car, career, relationships, and leisure activities, and immerse yourself in the emotions of joy, gratitude, and satisfaction that accompany your success.
- **Use Affirmations:** Incorporate affirmations into your daily routine to reinforce positive

beliefs and intentions related to wealth and prosperity. Write down affirmations that affirm your financial goals, such as "I am abundant in all areas of my life," "Money flows to me effortlessly and abundantly," or "I am worthy of wealth and success." Repeat these affirmations aloud or silently throughout the day, allowing them to sink into your subconscious mind and replace limiting beliefs with empowering ones.

- **Create Vision Boards:** Create a vision board or digital vision board that visually represents your financial goals and aspirations. Gather images, quotes, and symbols that symbolize abundance, success, and prosperity, and arrange them on your vision board in a way that inspires and motivates you. Place your vision board in a prominent location where you can see it daily, and spend time visualizing your goals and affirming your intentions as you gaze upon it.

PRACTICE SELF-DISCIPLINE & DELAY GRATIFICATION

Self-discipline & Delayed gratification are essential qualities for mastering the wealth mindset and achieving long-term financial success. By exercising self-control, resisting impulses, and prioritizing long-term goals over short-term pleasures, you can build wealth steadily over time. Here's how to practice self-discipline and delayed gratification:

- ***Set Clear Goals:*** Set clear, specific, and meaningful financial goals that align with your values, priorities, and aspirations. Break down your goals into smaller, manageable tasks and create a plan of action for achieving them. Establish deadlines and milestones to track your progress and hold yourself accountable to your goals.

- **Create a Budget:** Develop a budget that reflects your financial goals and helps you allocate your resources effectively. Track your income and expenses, identify areas for saving and investing, and prioritize spending on essentials and high-value items that align with your long-term objectives. Use your budget as a tool for practicing self-discipline and making intentional financial decisions.
- **Avoid Impulsive Spending:** Practice mindfulness and self-awareness when it comes to spending money, and avoid giving in to impulse purchases or lifestyle inflation. Pause and reflect before making discretionary purchases, and ask yourself whether the item aligns with your values and goals, or if it's a fleeting desire driven by impulse or emotional spending. Cultivate the habit of delaying gratification and

saving towards meaningful goals rather than succumbing to immediate wants.

- **Reward Yourself Strategically:** While practicing delayed gratification, it's also important to reward yourself strategically for achieving milestones and making progress towards your goals. Set up small rewards or incentives that motivate you to stay disciplined and on track, such as treating yourself to a special meal, experience, or purchase after reaching a savings goal or completing a significant task.
- **Surround Yourself with Success:** Surrounding yourself with success involves cultivating a supportive environment and surrounding yourself with people, resources, and influences that inspire and uplift you on your journey to financial success. By seeking out positive role models, mentors, and peers who embody the wealth mindset and

success principles, you can accelerate your own growth and achievement. Here's how to surround yourself with success.

- **Seek Out Mentors and Role Models:** Identify mentors, role models, and successful individuals who have achieved the level of success you aspire to and seek their guidance, advice, and inspiration. Learn from their experiences, strategies, and insights, and model their behaviors and habits that contribute to their success. Surround yourself with positive influences that motivate you to stretch your limits and pursue your goals with passion and determination.

- **Join Supportive Community:** Join communities, networking groups, or mastermind programs where you can connect with like-minded individuals who share your goals and aspirations. Surround yourself with a supportive community of peers who encourage, challenge, and uplift you, and provide accountability and camaraderie on your journey to financial success. Engage in meaningful conversations, share resources and experiences, and collaborate on projects or initiatives that align with your goals.

- **Consume Inspirational Contents:** Immerse yourself in inspirational content, such as books, podcasts, videos, and seminars, that inspire and motivate you to achieve your financial goals. Seek out content that aligns with your values, interests, and aspirations, and exposes you to new ideas, perspectives, and strategies for success. Invest in your personal and professional development by dedicating time each day to consuming uplifting and educational content that nourishes your mind and spirit.

- **Limit Negative Influences:** Be mindful of negative influences and toxic environments that undermine your confidence, motivation, and well-being. Surround yourself with positive energy and people who support your growth and success, and limit exposure to negativity, criticism, and pessimism. Protect your mental and emotional health by setting boundaries and distancing yourself from individuals or environments that drain your energy or detract from your goals.

~Chapter 13~

Conclusion

Embracing the Journey to Financial Freedom

The journey to financial freedom is not merely about accumulating wealth; it's a transformative process that involves cultivating a mindset of abundance, adopting empowering beliefs and behaviors, and aligning your actions with your financial goals and aspirations. As we conclude our exploration of achieving wealth through mindset, it's essential to reflect on the lessons learned, commit to continuous growth, and inspire others to embark on their own journey towards financial freedom.

Reflecting on Your Progress

Take a moment to reflect on your progress and achievements thus far in your journey towards financial freedom. Celebrate the milestones you've reached, the challenges you've overcome, and the lessons you've learned along the way. Recognize the growth and transformation you've experienced, both personally and financially, and acknowledge the efforts and dedication you've invested in pursuing your goals.

Reflect on the mindset shifts and behavioral changes you've made to cultivate a wealth mindset and align your actions with your financial aspirations. Consider the challenges you've faced, the setbacks you've encountered, and the strategies you've employed to navigate adversity and stay focused on your goals. Use these reflections as a source of motivation and inspiration to continue moving forward on your path to financial freedom.

Committing to Continuous Growth

Commit to a lifelong journey of continuous growth and learning in your pursuit of financial freedom. Recognize that achieving wealth is not a destination but a dynamic and evolving process that requires ongoing effort, adaptation, and refinement. Stay curious, open-minded, and proactive in seeking out new opportunities, acquiring new knowledge and skills, and expanding your horizons.

Embrace challenges as opportunities for growth and view setbacks as valuable learning experiences that propel you forward on your journey. Be willing to step outside your comfort zone, take calculated risks, and embrace uncertainty as a catalyst for personal and financial growth. Cultivate resilience, perseverance, and a growth mindset that empowers you to overcome obstacles and thrive in the face of adversity.

Inspiring Others to Achieve Wealth

As you continue your journey towards financial freedom, strive to inspire and empower others to embark on their own path towards prosperity. Share your experiences, insights, and lessons learned with those around you, and encourage them to cultivate a wealth mindset and take proactive steps towards achieving their financial goals. Be a role model for financial empowerment and success, leading by example and demonstrating the transformative power of mindset in shaping one's financial destiny.

Support and uplift others on their journey by offering encouragement, guidance, and resources to help them overcome obstacles and stay focused on their goals. Foster a culture of collaboration, mutual support, and abundance consciousness within your community, workplace, or social circle, where individuals can come together to share ideas, exchange knowledge, and support each other's growth and success.

By inspiring and empowering others to achieve wealth through mindset, you contribute to a ripple effect of positive change and transformation that extends far beyond your own life. Together, we can create a world where financial freedom is accessible to all, and where individuals are empowered to realize their full potential and live a life of abundance, fulfillment, and purpose.

As we draw the curtains on our journey towards cultivating a wealthy mindset, let us pause to reflect on the profound transformations we've undergone and the limitless possibilities that lie ahead. In this concluding chapter, we reaffirm our belief in the abundance of life and the power of our minds to shape our destiny. We remind ourselves that wealth is not just about material possessions but a mindset—a legacy that transcends generations and leaves an indelible mark on the world.

Remember, You Deserve to Be Rich

The journey to wealth begins with a simple yet powerful realization: You deserve to be rich. It's not about entitlement or luck but recognizing your inherent worth and embracing the abundance that surrounds you. In this section, we reaffirm your right to financial success and challenge any lingering doubts or fears that may hold you back from claiming your rightful place among the prosperous.

Imagine standing in front of a mirror, gazing into your own eyes, and declaring with unwavering conviction, "I deserve to be rich." Feel the truth of these words reverberate through your entire being, igniting a fire of determination and possibility within you. With this newfound belief firmly rooted in your mind, you embark on a journey of abundance, knowing that the universe is conspiring in your favor to manifest your wildest dreams.

Replace scarcity with abundance. You are worthy of financial security and the freedom to pursue your passions. Wealth creation is not a privilege reserved for the chosen few; it's a journey available to anyone willing to commit and learn. Believe in yourself, your abilities, and the power of your financial plan.

Living a Life of Abundance Starts Now!

Don't wait until you reach a certain number in your bank account to start living abundantly. Here's how to cultivate abundance in every aspect of your life:

- **Practice Gratitude:** Appreciate the good things you already have, big or small.

Gratitude fosters *a sense of abundance and attracts more* positivity into your life.
- **Give Back to Others:** Sharing your resources with those in need is a powerful way to experience abundance. Volunteer your time, donate to charity, or simply mentor someone less fortunate.
- **Invest in Yourself:** Your greatest asset is yourself. Invest in your education, skills, and personal growth. The more valuable you become, the greater your earning potential.
- **Pursue Your Passions:** Don't let financial worries hold you back from what truly matters. Find ways to incorporate your passions into your life, even if it starts small.

Remember, financial freedom is a journey, not a destination.

There will be bumps along the road, but with unwavering self-belief, a commitment to your plan, and the support of a positive community, you can achieve your financial goals and live a life filled with abundance.

The journey to financial freedom is a deeply personal and transformative experience that involves cultivating a wealth mindset, embracing growth and learning, and inspiring others to pursue their own path to prosperity. As you continue on your journey, remember to reflect on your progress, commit to continuous growth, and empower others to achieve wealth through mindset. By doing so, you not only transform your own life but also contribute to a more prosperous and abundant world for all.

Finally, as we bid farewell to the pages of this book, let us carry forth the lessons learned and the wisdom gained into every aspect of our lives. May we continue to cultivate a wealthy mindset, not just for ourselves but for future generations to come. And may we never forget that abundance is not just a destination but a journey—a legacy for life that begins anew with each passing moment. As you step boldly into the future, may you do so with the unwavering belief that you are destined for greatness and the unshakeable conviction that the best is yet to come.

Remember, you are the author of your financial story.

With the knowledge, tools, and unwavering mindset gained from this guide, you have the power to rewrite your financial narrative and create a legacy of abundance for yourself and future generations. Embrace the journey, stay committed, and live a life filled with financial freedom and fulfillment!

www.ingramcontent.com/pod-product-compliance
Lightning Source LLC
Chambersburg PA
CBHW071510220526
45472CB00003B/968